The Titanic

by Michael Burgan

Content Adviser: Karen Kamuda,
Vice President, Titanic Historical Society and Titanic Museum,
Indian Orchard, Massachusetts

Reading Adviser: Dr. Linda D. Labbo,
Department of Reading Education, College of Education,
The University of Georgia

COMPASS POINT BOOKS
MINNEAPOLIS, MINNESOTA

Compass Point Books
3109 West 50th Street, #115
Minneapolis, MN 55410

Visit Compass Point Books on the Internet at *www.compasspointbooks.com*
or e-mail your request to *custserv@compasspointbooks.com*

On the cover: The *Titanic* sets off from Southampton on her maiden voyage.
Photograph taken April 10, 1912, by local resident H. G. Lloyd.

Photographs ©: Ralph White/Corbis, cover, 7 (all), 10, 14, 15, 38, 41; Christie's Images/Corbis, 4;
Hulton/Archive by Getty Images, 5, 21, 25, 26, 30, 31, 32; Corbis, 8; The Pierpont Morgan
Library/Art Resource N.Y., 9; Leonard de Selva/Corbis, 11; The Mariners' Museum, Newport
News, VA, 12, 28; Bettmann/Corbis, 17, 33, 36; Fr. Browne, S.J., Collection, 18, 22; Courtesy
Henning Pfeifer, 23; AFP/Getty Images, 29, 39, 40; North Wind Picture Archives, 35; Reuters
NewMedia Inc./Corbis, 37.

Editor: Catherine Neitge
Photo Researcher: Svetlana Zhurkina
Designer/Page Production: Bradfordesign, Inc./Biner Design
Cartographer: XNR Productions, Inc.

Library of Congress Cataloging-in-Publication Data
Burgan, Michael.
The Titanic / by Michael Burgan.
      p. cm. — (We the people)
   Summary: A history of the Titanic and a recounting of one of the worst maritime disasters
in history.
   Includes index.
   ISBN 0-7565-0614-X (hardcover)
   ISBN 0-7565-1045-7 (paperback)
   1. Titanic (Steamship)—Juvenile literature. 2. Shipwrecks—North Atlantic Ocean—Juvenile
literature. [1. Titanic (Steamship) 2. Shipwrecks.] I. Title. II. Series: We the people (Compass
Point Books)
   G530.T6B85 2004
   910'.9163'4—dc22   2003014442

TABLE OF CONTENTS

NOTE: *In this book, words that are defined in the glossary are in* **bold** *the first time they appear in the text.*

DISASTER ON THE SEA

On the night of April 14, 1912, the Royal Mail Steamer (R.M.S.) *Titanic* cut through the icy waters of the North Atlantic Ocean. The *Titanic* was the largest and grandest ship of its time. On this maiden, or first, voyage, the ship carried more than 2,200 passengers and crew. By 11:30 P.M., most of the passengers had already gone to their cabins for the night. Only a few stayed up to play cards and chat.

A poster advertised travel on the White Star Line's Titanic *and its sister ship, the* Olympic.

4

In parts of the ship, however, crew members were still on duty. Some ran the giant steam boilers that powered the *Titanic*. In front of the **bridge,** on a tall pole called a mast, two sailors in the **crow's nest** watched for any signs of trouble. They did not see the danger lurking in the water until it was too late.

Before the *Titanic* left Southampton, England, for New York, its builders called the ship "practically unsinkable." They had used the most modern shipbuilding technology of the day. But when the *Titanic* brushed along a huge iceberg that night at sea, its sides could not take the pressure. **Rivet**

Tugboats pull the Titanic *as it leaves Belfast, Ireland, where it was built.*

heads broke off and large steel plates bent. As the plates moved, water flowed into the lower levels of the ship. Within three hours, the *Titanic* sank with many people still onboard.

The sinking of the *Titanic* was one of the world's worst **maritime** disasters. People from many countries died. Some were among the wealthiest Americans of the day. Others were Europeans looking to start a new life in the United States. Children lost their parents, and wives lost their husbands.

The disaster led to important changes in maritime safety. It also showed how bravely people can behave in difficult times. Instead of entering lifeboats, some passengers stayed onboard to help others leave. Officers and crew members kept working, knowing they faced almost certain death. The story of the *Titanic* has inspired many movies and books. Interest in the *Titanic* grew after 1985, when scientists found the remains of the ship on the bottom of the Atlantic Ocean. Today, the *Titanic* story points out that technology is not perfect and even the best-trained people can make deadly mistakes.

A scientist holds a cherub statue that was recovered from the elegant grand staircase of the Titanic, shown above.

BUILDING THE BEST EVER

At the beginning of the 20th century, travelers had to sail on steamships to cross the Atlantic Ocean. (Plane flights over long distances were still years away.) Passengers could choose from a number of different steamships. The biggest and fastest belonged to two shipping companies: the Cunard Line and the White Star Line.

The Cunard Line's Lusitania *arrives in New York in 1907.*

8

In 1907, Cunard launched the *Lusitania*. At the time, it was the world's largest passenger ship. A sister ship, the *Mauretania,* was almost identical. J. Bruce Ismay was the chairman and managing director of the White Star Line. He planned to build three ocean liners larger than the Cunard vessels. J. P. Morgan, a wealthy American whose

J.P. Morgan's company owned the White Star Line.

company owned the White Star Line, went along with the plan. Morgan had made a fortune in banking and railroads, and he was one of the richest men in the world. He was eager to defeat rival shipping companies, especially Cunard. The new White Star ocean liners were named *Olympic, Titanic,* and *Britannic.*

The Titanic *was built at the Harland and Wolff shipyards in Belfast.*

Work on the *Titanic* began in March 1909 at a ship-yard in Belfast, Ireland. Three years later, the largest ship of its time was ready to sail. The *Titanic* was almost 900 feet (274 meters) long and weighed more than 46,000 tons (41,400 metric tons). Just one anchor on the giant ship weighed more than 15 tons (13.5 metric tons). Inside, the ship could carry up to 2,600 passengers, while almost 1,000 crew members kept it running.

The *Titanic* was not quite as fast as the *Lusitania* and its sister ship. Instead, Ismay and the ship's designer, Thomas Andrews, wanted their ship to be luxurious and comfortable. At the time, rooms inside steamships were divided into three classes. Passengers paid more to travel first class, less for second and third. On the *Titanic,* the cabins and public rooms for first-class passengers looked like the insides of Europe's finest hotels. The best materials were used to decorate the

A poster advertising the soap given to first-class passengers shows the Titanic's *interior.*

first-class areas. Other features included a gym, a library, and an indoor pool. One magazine reported that the *Titanic* offered "passenger **accommodation** of unrivalled…

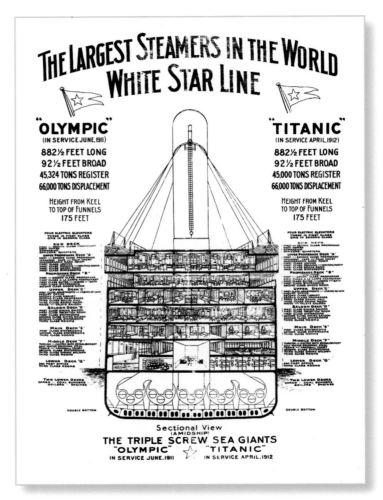

A cross-sectional drawing of the White Star Line's famous ships

magnificence." Accommodations for second- and third-class passengers topped those found on other ships as well.

The *Titanic* also boasted the latest safety features. The lower decks of the ship were divided into 16 **compartments.** Separating them were watertight doors. If water entered one compartment, the doors would shut and keep the water from entering the entire ship. The *Titanic* was designed to stay afloat even if water filled the two largest of the watertight compartments.

The ship also had what was then a new invention: wireless radio. The "wireless" let the operators send and receive messages in **Morse code.** Using these electronic signals, the *Titanic* could communicate with radio operators onshore or on other ships.

Despite these features, the *Titanic* and every other large steamship were short of one important safety item: lifeboats. The *Titanic* carried 20—more than British regulations required, but not nearly enough to hold everyone onboard.

THE SHIP SAILS

On Wednesday, April 10, 1912, the *Titanic* was ready for its maiden voyage. Captain Edward J. Smith was in charge of the ship. He had worked for the White Star Line for more than 25 years. Smith's nickname was the Millionaire's Captain. The passengers who sailed on White Star ships enjoyed his pleasant personality.

Captain Edward J. Smith (right) and another officer stand on the Titanic's *deck. The Rev. F. M. Browne, who took the photo, got off the ship in Ireland, three days before it sank.*

The Titanic *sets off on her maiden—and final—voyage from Southampton, England.*

The *Titanic* sailed from Southampton, England, then made brief stops in France and Ireland before heading across the Atlantic. Along with the passengers and crew, totaling 2,201 people, the ship carried mail and cargo bound for New York. Some of the wealthiest of the first-class passengers traveled with their servants. A few brought along their dogs. The ship had kennels for pets, but at least one passenger kept her dog in her cabin.

The list of famous people onboard included John Jacob Astor, a wealthy New York real estate developer, and Isidor Straus, founder of the Macy's department store. Other millionaires included George Widener of Philadelphia and Margaret "Molly" Brown of Colorado. A noted figure was Major Archibald Butt, who was President William Howard Taft's military adviser. J. Bruce Ismay was onboard, eager to see if the *Titanic* would perform as well as her sister *Olympic* had the year before. J. P. Morgan was supposed to make the voyage but canceled because of business.

The *Titanic*'s sailing got off to a rough start. Leaving the dock in Southampton, the ship almost collided with the *New York,* another passenger ship. The *New York* was tied to the dock but broke loose as the *Titanic* passed. The two ships missed each other by just

Margaret "Molly" Brown of Colorado became known as the unsinkable Molly Brown.

a few feet. One passenger said, "That's a bad **omen.**" Most passengers, however, soon forgot about the near-miss and prepared to enjoy their trip.

Exercise machines were part of the Titanic's *well-equipped gym.*

The voyage across the North Atlantic went smoothly. The seas were calm on an ocean known for fierce storms. One passenger later wrote, "I enjoyed myself as if I were in a summer palace on the seashore, surrounded by every comfort." Each day, Captain Smith increased the ship's speed closer to its limit of 23 **knots** (26.4 miles per hour).

Not everything went perfectly, however. A small fire had been burning in the coal room since the *Titanic* had left England. The coal was the fuel used in the large boilers that created the steam to power the ship's engines. The crew needed four days to put out the fire. Also, three nights after setting sail, the wireless radio broke down for a few hours, but the operators were able to fix it. And the *Titanic* had received reports of large ice fields. Icebergs and smaller pieces of ice were common in the North Atlantic in April. That year, however, the ice was farther south than usual. The warnings from other ships increased as the *Titanic* neared North America.

"ICEBERG RIGHT AHEAD"

On the night of April 14, the *Titanic* continued to steam along at just under 23 knots. That day, Captain Smith had received more reports of ice, so he took a step to lower the

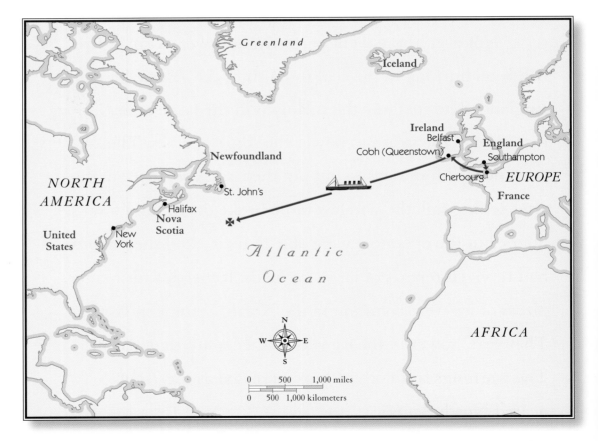

A map of the Titanic's *doomed voyage*

risk of hitting an ice field. Usually, as ships approached Newfoundland, Canada, they cut southwest before heading west for the United States. Smith sent the *Titanic* even farther south than normal before taking the turn west. With this move, he hoped to miss any icebergs drifting down from the north.

Captain Edward J. Smith

The weather that night was cold, clear, and calm. The stars shined, and one of the ship's officers hoped their light would reflect off any icebergs that might be in the water. Around 9 P.M., Smith visited the bridge before going to his cabin for the night. He left Second Officer Charles Lightoller in charge. In case of any trouble, Smith

21

told him, "Let me know at once. I shall just be inside."
Lightoller told the two lookouts outside to watch carefully
for icebergs.

Radio operator Jack Phillips died in the disaster.

In the radio room, Jack Phillips tried to keep up with all the messages coming in. He also had a stack of messages from *Titanic* passengers waiting to be sent. A little after 9:30 P.M., Phillips received another message about an ice field—one directly in the ship's path. The radio operator, however, did not send the message to the bridge. He was overworked with many passengers' messages and put it aside for Harold Bride, the other operator, to bring up. The message, however, got lost in the pile.

22

At 10 P.M., First Officer William Murdoch took command of the ship. The *Titanic* was still traveling at almost 23 knots. Two new lookouts took their position in the crow's nest. Just before 11:40 P.M., one of them noticed a dark shape in the water. He rang the crow's nest bell and telephoned the bridge: "Iceberg right ahead."

The only known photo of what experts believe is the iceberg that hit the Titanic *has come to light. It was taken by a Czech seaman five days after the tragedy and recently discovered by a German journalist.*

At almost the same time, Murdoch saw the berg. He ordered that the ship turn hard to the starboard, or right, and that the engines be reversed. The **bow** of the *Titanic* missed the berg, but under the water's surface, the ship scraped along the ice. At the same time, pieces of ice broke off the berg, falling into the forward well deck.

Throughout the ship, only a few people heard the scraping noise or felt the slight jolt of steel hitting ice. In one of the boiler rooms, however, the crew saw water pouring into the ship. The water flowed through more than 300 feet (91 m) of damaged hull on the ship's front starboard side. The watertight doors on the ship shut, but water was filling five of the ship's watertight compartments.

Captain Smith had felt the ship strike the iceberg, and he soon learned about the water rushing into the *Titanic*. He knew he would have less than two hours to get the passengers into lifeboats before the ship sank. He also knew that he lacked enough boats for the task.

24

This 1912 illustration shows how the Titanic *scraped an iceberg under the water's surface.*

MATTERS OF LIFE AND DEATH

News about the iceberg soon spread around the ship.
The crew prepared the passengers to abandon the *Titanic*.
Many could not believe that the ship was in danger.

The Titanic *did not have enough lifeboats to carry all of its passengers.*

26

"What do they need of lifeboats?" one woman asked. "This ship could smash a hundred icebergs and not feel it." But just one iceberg had been enough to put the lives of more than 2,200 people in danger.

Out on deck, passengers stood in the freezing night air waiting to board the boats. Despite the danger, few people panicked as the *Titanic* started to sink. One survivor later said, "The passengers were so little alarmed that they joked over the matter." Meanwhile, the ship's band played to lift the spirits of the passengers as they prepared to leave.

At the lifeboat stations, women and children were supposed to board first. Some men, however, did manage to scramble into a few of the boats before they were launched. At times, the boats left half-empty, if no women and children were at that station. This, of course, proved to be a terrible mistake, since more lives could have been saved. Husbands kissed their wives and children goodbye, and a few wives refused to leave their husband's side.

Women and children were loaded onto the lifeboats first.

Molly Brown, the Colorado millionaire, won fame for helping other women onto boats, refusing to board one herself. Two men finally had to put her into a lifeboat. As the lifeboats rowed through the icy water, the passengers could see the *Titanic* sinking deeper into the ocean.

While the passengers were being helped off, Smith had the radio operators send out a C.Q.D., the message for **distress.** The crew also launched signal rockets. Out in the

The ship Olympic *reported in a telegraph message that it had received* Titanic's *distress signal.*

distance, several ships heard the call for help and began to steam toward the *Titanic*. The closest was the *Carpathia,* but it was still 58 miles (93 kilometers) away. Another ship, the *Californian,* was even closer. Its radio, however, was not on. The operator had shut down his wireless for the night just minutes before the *Titanic* sent its first distress message.

Below decks, the engineers kept the engines running. The engines provided power for lights and the pumps trying to empty the watertight compartments. The water, however, continued to flood in. Around 2 A.M., the ship's

stern began to rise out of the ocean, as the bow continued to plunge below the water's surface. With the last lifeboats gone, some passengers dove into the freezing ocean. Some were rescued by the lifeboats. At about 2:20 A.M., the *Titanic* broke in half, then completely sank into the Atlantic. Hundreds of passengers and crew were still onboard the doomed ship.

An illustration from a 1912 London newspaper shows survivors watching the Titanic *plunging beneath the sea.*

Shortly after 4 A.M. the *Carpathia* arrived and began pulling the survivors out of the lifeboats. One passenger later said, "The hours that elapsed before we were picked up by the *Carpathia* were the longest and most terrible that I ever spent." Most of the survivors were exhausted and freezing; some had suffered frostbite. More than 1,500 people had died, while only 705 people survived the sinking. In the days that followed, other ships patrolled the site of the collision. Their sailors removed nearly 400 dead bodies from the water.

A Titanic lifeboat is hoisted aboard the rescue ship Carpathia

AFTER THE DISASTER

Around the world, people could not believe that the great *Titanic* was lost at sea. Officials in the United States and Great Britain held hearings to find out exactly what happened. Some people wondered if Captain Smith should

A London newsboy sells copies of the Evening News with its story of the Titanic *disaster.*

have slowed down the ship, since he knew there was ice in the area. Second Officer Lightoller defended Smith's decision to maintain speed. He said most captains would have done the same thing under the conditions. William Alden Smith, a U.S. senator from Michigan, asked if the ship had enough lifeboats. The answer, of course, was no, but the White Star Line had not broken any laws.

Captain Stanley Lord of the *Californian* received some of the toughest questions. Some of his crew had

J. Bruce Ismay (facing the camera) testified at U.S. Senate hearings that investigated the Titanic *tragedy.*

seen the lights of an unknown ship the night of the sinking. They had also seen rockets. Lord knew the *Titanic* was in the region, but the ship he saw earlier seemed too small to be that huge vessel. His crew tried to send Morse code messages by flashing lights, but they never received a response. Senator Smith and others blamed Lord for not sailing toward the rockets. Over the years, some people have tried to defend Lord. They claim a second ship was near the *Californian* that night, and Lord had not seen the *Titanic*.

After the *Titanic* sinking, some people wondered if the first- and second-class passengers had received special treatment the night of April 14. A large percentage of these passengers survived the sinking, compared to the number of third-class passengers. For a time, a rumor spread that the third-class passengers had been locked in their part of the ship. The rumor was not true. But these passengers did have farther to go to reach the lifeboats. That distance may explain why fewer of them were saved.

34

Survivors of the Titanic *tragedy crowd the deck of the* Carpathia. *The disaster spurred new regulations for passenger ships.*

After the investigations, government officials took action. In the future, every passenger ship would carry enough lifeboats for everyone on board. Passengers would have to go through a drill to make sure they knew what to do during an emergency. Ships were also required to keep their radios operating 24 hours a day. In 1913, the major

A U.S. Coast Guard International Ice Patrol ship reports on icebergs in the North Atlantic.

maritime countries created the International Ice Patrol. Its job was to find and track icebergs in the North Atlantic.

Over the years, films and books on the *Titanic* disaster began to appear. A 1930 movie about a ship called "Atlantic" was based on the *Titanic* disaster. Several other films about the ship were also made. In 1955, author Walter Lord published *A Night to Remember*. Lord interviewed more than 60 survivors of the sinking. His book gave most people their first detailed look at the *Titanic* sinking. A film based on the book was released in 1958.

THE GREAT DISCOVERY

By the 1970s, engineers and scientists had created small vessels called **submersibles** that could explore the ocean floor.

American scientist Robert D. Ballard wanted to use these subs to locate the wreck of the *Titanic*. Ballard spent more than 10 years organizing an **expedition** to locate the ship.

To find the *Titanic,* Ballard used special remote-control submersibles that he designed. From a ship on the surface, Ballard

Robert D. Ballard spent years organizing a search for the Titanic.

37

The ship's crew prepares to launch the Argo.

and his crew controlled a submersible called *Argo*. Inside *Argo* was a remote-controlled robot called Jason. The robot carried lights and a video camera that sent images of the ocean floor to Ballard. Once Ballard knew the general area of the wreck, he put *Argo* and Jason to work. Finally, on September 1, 1985, Ballard and his crew spotted one of the *Titanic*'s huge boilers. The wreck was more than two miles (three kilometers) below the water's surface. Ballard and his crew celebrated, but then they remembered the horrors of April 14, 1912. Ballard later wrote that he could imagine "the ghostly shapes of the lifeboats and the piercing shouts and screams of people freezing to death in the water."

In 1986, Ballard returned to examine the wreck more closely. This time he used a submersible called *Alvin* and a robot named Jason Jr. The robot's cameras recorded the first detailed look of the wreck and the insides of the *Titanic*. Ballard and his crew clearly saw the two pieces of the ship. On the ocean bottom, they saw such things as wine bottles and a doll's head.

Jason Jr. leaves the submersible Alvin *and prepares to shoot photos of the* Titanic.

Since Ballard's discovery, more people have made expeditions to the *Titanic* site. Sometimes people film the sunken ship. Other people come searching for **artifacts**. Several thousands have been recovered so far. These include pieces of jewelry, luggage, and silver plates. In 1999, a Russian sub brought several tourists to the site. They paid $35,000 each to spend one night on the sub as it landed on the *Titanic* wreck.

One of the visitors to the *Titanic* was filmmaker James Cameron. In 1997, he had released a movie about the disaster. Using computers and models, Cameron was able to show what the *Titanic* looked like during its brief voyage. He also showed the details of the sinking. His film "Titanic"

A scene from the movie "Titanic," which won 11 Academy Awards

was one of the most successful movies ever made. It received 11 Academy Awards—the highest honor in the film industry. The film also sparked new interest in the *Titanic* disaster.

Today, scientists and others still visit the wreck of the *Titanic*. Eventually, the remains will disappear. Tiny sea creatures eat away at the metal, and sand covers up some of the artifacts. Even when the ship is gone, however, the story of the *Titanic* will live on, fascinating people all over the world.

The bow of the Titanic *rests on the ocean floor.*

41

GLOSSARY

accommodation—a cabin fitted out for passengers

artifacts—human-made objects found at historical sites

bow—the very front of a ship

bridge—the control center high on the forward section of a ship

compartments—sections of a ship between two bulkheads, which are watertight walls stretching from one side of the ship to the other

crow's nest—platform near the top of a ship's mast

distress—in urgent need of help

expedition—a long journey made for a special purpose

knot—an international nautical unit of speed equal to 6,076 feet (1,853 meters) per hour; a British knot is 6,080 feet (1,854 m) per hour

maritime—related to the sea, ships, or sea travel

Morse code—a system of signaling using dots and dashes sent as sound or light

omen—a sign of something that will happen in the future

rivet—a metal bolt or pin used to hold together metal

stern—the back end of a ship

submersibles—small vessels used under water, usually for research

DID YOU KNOW?

- The food onboard the *Titanic* included more than 120,000 pounds (54,480 kilograms) of meat and fish, 10,000 pounds (4,540 kg) of sugar, and 1,500 gallons (5,677 liters) of milk.

- The artifacts found at the *Titanic* site include a child's model airplane kit, playing cards, and gold jewelry.

- Molly Brown of Colorado, one of the heroes of the disaster, was later the subject of a hit musical called "The Unsinkable Molly Brown."

- Edward Kamuda established the Titanic Historical Society in 1963 in Massachusetts to preserve *Titanic* history. The Ulster Titanic Society was founded in Belfast, Northern Ireland, to research the *Titanic* and the shipyard where it was built. There are many *Titanic* groups throughout the world.

IMPORTANT DATES

Timeline

1907	The Cunard Line launches the *Lusitania*, which at the time was the world's largest ship
1909	The White Star Line begins construction of the *Titanic*
1912	The *Titanic* sails on April 10; the ship hits an iceberg late on the night of April 14; the *Titanic* sinks early on April 15
1913	The International Ice Patrol is formed to track icebergs in the North Atlantic Ocean
1955	Walter Lord publishes *A Night to Remember,* a book on the *Titanic* disaster
1985	Robert Ballard discovers the wreck of the *Titanic*
1986	Ballard takes the first detailed pictures and video of the wreck
1997	The movie "Titanic" is released and becomes one of the most successful films of all time

44

IMPORTANT PEOPLE

JOHN JACOB ASTOR (1864–1912)
Member of a rich and famous American family, he died during the sinking of the Titanic

ROBERT BALLARD (1942–)
Scientist who discovered the wreck of the Titanic *in 1985*

MARGARET "MOLLY" TOBIN BROWN (1867–1932)
Humanitarian and socialite who survived the sinking of the Titanic

JOSEPH BRUCE ISMAY (1862–1937)
Chairman and managing director of the White Star Line who first proposed building the Titanic

STANLEY LORD (1877–1962)
Captain of the Californian, *the ship that some people believe was closest to the* Titanic *when it struck an iceberg*

JOHN PIERPONT MORGAN (1837–1913)
American financier and owner of the White Star Line

EDWARD J. SMITH (1850–1912)
Captain of the Titanic

WANT TO KNOW MORE?

At the Library

Adams, Simon. *Titanic.* New York: DK Publishing, 1999.

Harmon, Daniel E. *The Titanic.* Philadelphia: Chelsea House Publishers, 2001.

Hill, Christine M. *Robert Ballard: Oceanographer Who Discovered the Titanic.* Berkeley Heights, N.J.: Enslow Publishers, 1999.

Marschall, Ken. *Inside the Titanic.* Boston: Little, Brown, 1997.

Ruffin, Frances E. *"Unsinkable" Molly Brown.* New York: Rosen Publishing Group, 2002.

On the Web

For more information on the *Titanic,* use FactHound

to track down Web sites related to this book.

1. Go to *www.compasspointbooks.com/facthound*

2. Type in this book ID: 075650614X

3. Click on the *Fetch It* button.

Your trusty FactHound will fetch the best Web sites for you!

Through the Mail

Titanic Historical Society

Box 51053

208 Main St.

Indian Orchard, MA 01151-0053

413/543-4770

To receive information from the world's largest *Titanic* organization

On the Road

The Molly Brown House Museum

1340 Pennsylvania St.

Denver, CO 80203

303/832-4092

To visit the home of the "unsinkable" Molly Brown

Maritime Museum of the Atlantic

1675 Lower Water St.

Halifax, Nova Scotia

Canada B3J 1S3

902/424-7490

To view an exhibit of *Titanic* artifacts and for information on Halifax cemeteries where many *Titanic* victims are buried

INDEX

About the Author

Michael Burgan is a freelance writer of books for children and adults. A history graduate of the University of Connecticut, he has written more than 60 fiction and nonfiction children's books for various publishers. For adult audiences, he has written news articles, essays, and plays. Michael Burgan is a recipient of an Educational Press Association of America award and belongs to the Society of Children's Book Writers and Illustrators.